SCHAUM D-THE ORANGE BOOK

Project Manager: Gail Lew

Cover Art: Martha Ramirez

From the Paramount Motion Picture "HATARI"

BABY ELEPHANT WALK

By HENRY MANCINI
Arranged by Wesley Schaum

EL03479A

AND I LOVE YOU SO

Words and Music by DON McLEAN
Arranged by Wesley Schaum

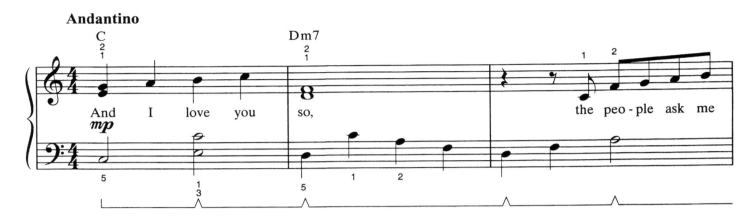

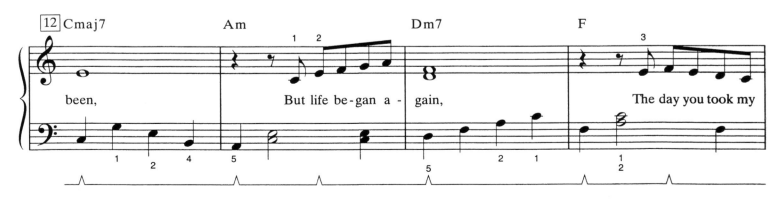

EL03479A

Theme Song from the Stanley Donen Production, a Universal Release

CHARADE

Lyric by JOHNNY MERCER

Music by HENRY MANCINI
Arranged by Wesley Schaum

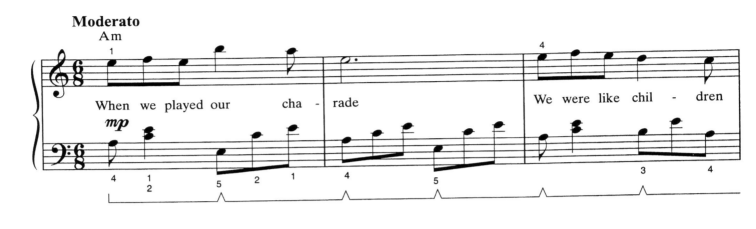

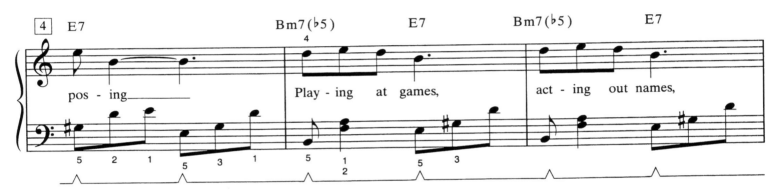

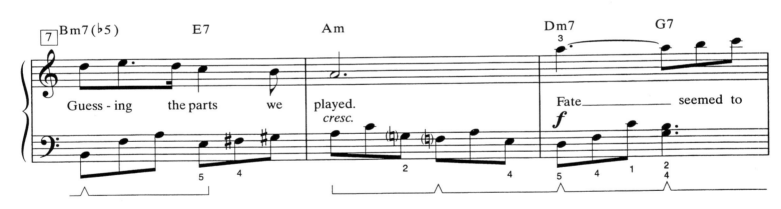

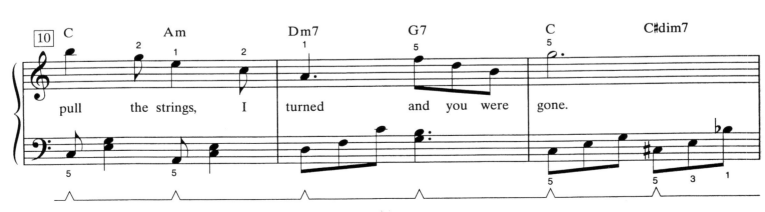

EL03479A

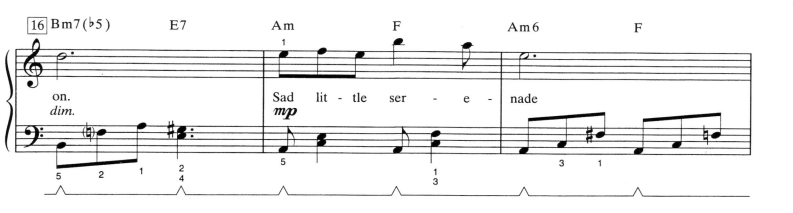
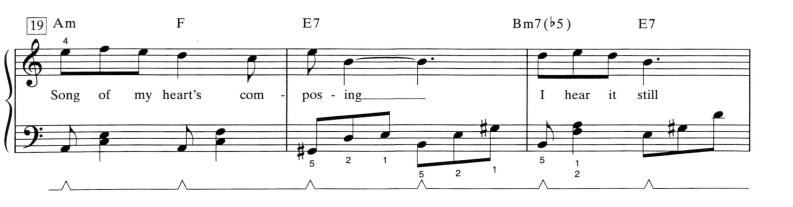
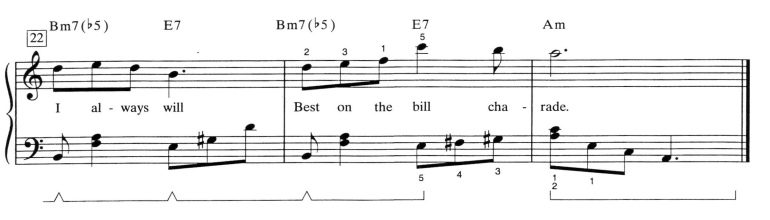

Columbia Pictures Presents an Ivan Reitman Film
A Black Rhino/Bernie Brillstein Production "GHOSTBUSTERS"

GHOSTBUSTERS

Words and Music by
RAY PARKER, JR.
Arranged by John W. Schaum

9

EL03479A

From The 20th Century-Fox Film "BUTCH CASSIDY AND THE SUNDANCE KID"

RAINDROPS KEEP FALLIN' ON MY HEAD

Words by HAL DAVID

Music by BURT BACHARACH
Arranged by Wesley Schaum

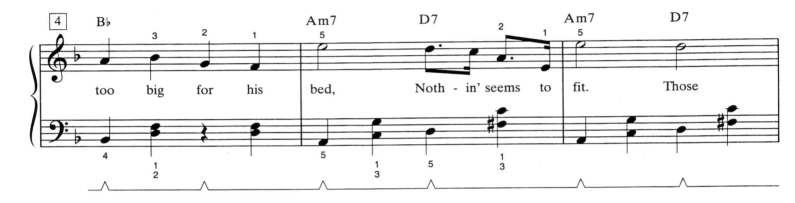

EL03479A

I HEARD IT THROUGH THE GRAPEVINE

Words and Music by
NORMAN WHITFIELD and BARRETT STRONG
Arranged by John W. Schaum

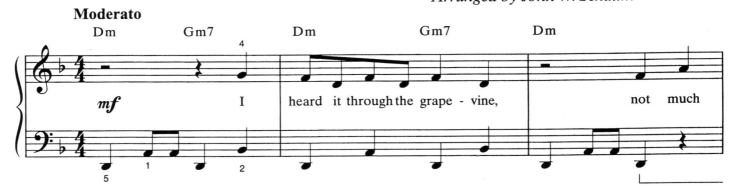

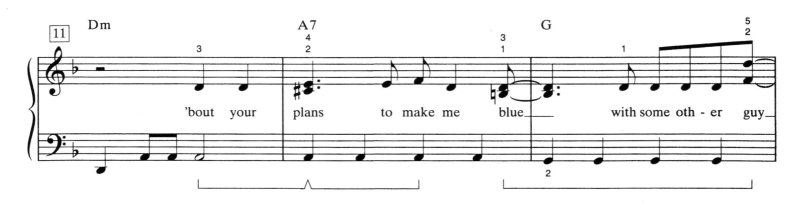

EL03479A

WHAT THE WORLD NEEDS NOW IS LOVE

Words by
HAL DAVID

Music by
BURT BACHARACH
Arranged by Wesley Schaum

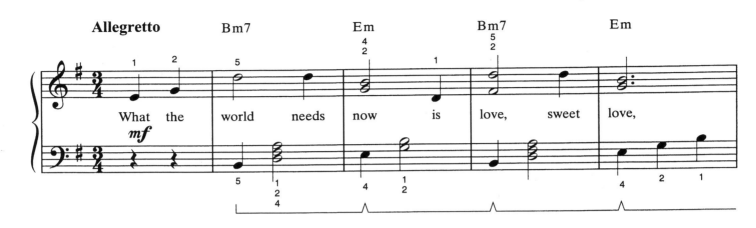

EL03479A

HEART AND SOUL

Words by
FRANK LOESSER

Music by
HOAGY CARMICHAEL
Arranged by Wesley Schaum

MISTY

Words by JOHNNY BURKE

Music by ERROLL GARNER
Arranged by John W. Schaum

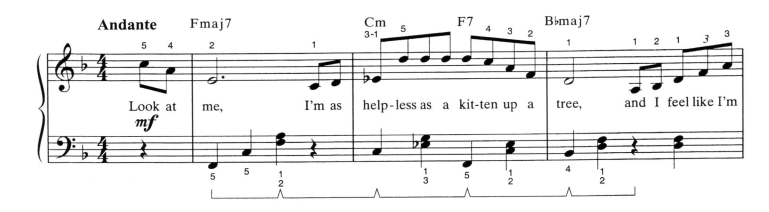

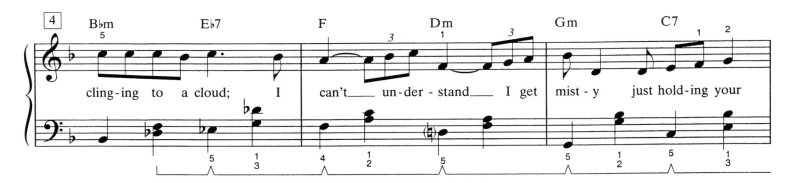

WITH YOU I'M BORN AGAIN

By CAROL CONNORS
and DAVID SHIRE
Arranged by Wesley Schaum

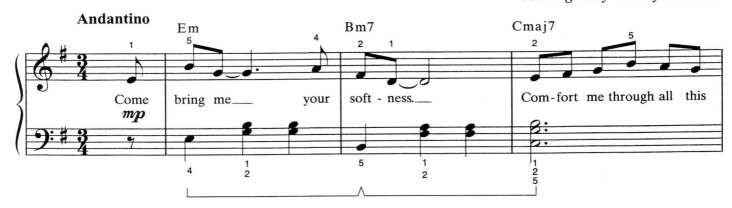

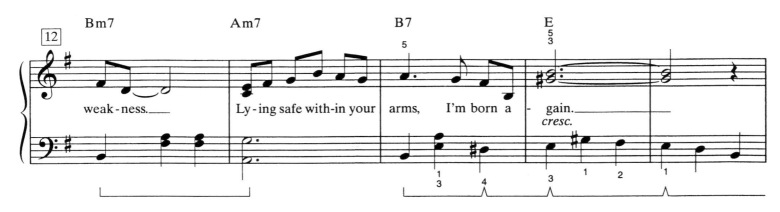

21

EL03479A

From the Motion Picture "DOCTOR DOLITTLE"

TALK TO THE ANIMALS

Words and Music by
LESLIE BRICUSSE
Arranged by Gail Lew